# The Power of Masterminding

## How to Soar to Success Effortlessly

MAC ATTRAM – ARTHUR MAGOULIANITI
KARL PEARSALL – STEVE W ROCHE

Published by Dragonwood
Published 2014

The Power of Masterminding

ISBN 978-0-9571826-6-0

**For more information visit www.masterminding.net.**

www.dragonwood.co.uk

# Contents

"You give before you get."

Napoleon Hill, Author of the best-selling book,
*'Think And Grow Rich'*

# WHY MAKE ACHIEVING SUCCESS SO DIFFICULT?

So what's with the geese on the front cover of this book, you may ask? Well, the fact is that there is much us humans can learn from the way that geese conduct themselves.

When they fly south in the autumn does each bird make its own way to warmer weather? They don't but, instead, they fly together in a particular V-formation.

The reason is that as each goose flaps its wings, it creates uplift for the birds that follow. By flying in this way as a group they have a 71% greater flying range than if each bird flew alone.

Also, if a goose falls out of formation, it suddenly feels the struggle of flying alone and quickly moves back into line to take advantage of the lifting power of the bird immediately in front of it.

The lesson that we can learn from this is that people who share a common direction, a sense of community and are willing to accept and give help can get to where they want to get to faster and with less effort and struggle because they will travel on the power of the whole group.

Another interesting fact is that when the lead goose gets tired, it moves back into the group and another goose takes its place at the front of the formation. From that we can learn that it pays dividends to take turns doing the hard work.

"Many of life's failures are people
who did not realize how close they were
to success when they gave up."

Thomas A. Edison

What's more, the geese flying in formation honk to encourage those ahead of them to keep going and also help and protect a goose if it gets sick or is wounded. Geese know that supporting each other improves the results achieved and recognize the value of standing by each other in difficult times.

If we now examine the lives of successful people throughout history we begin to see similar patterns.

Thomas Edison obtained 1,093 patents which is more than anyone else in history. Bill Gates created the world's most dominant software company. Henry Ford transformed the car industry.

So was their success entirely due to their own genius? Yes, these men made the most of their talents but they would never have achieved the level of success they did if they'd worked single-handedly.

You'll also notice that, very often, they started out facing tremendous obstacles and misfortunes. For example:

- Bill Gates was a college dropout
- Andrew Carnegie grew up in poverty
- Henry Ford was uneducated
- Arnold Schwarzenegger only spoke a few words of English when he arrived in the United States
- Helen Keller was unable to see, hear or speak

Again, what is interesting is that they didn't triumph over their challenges by themselves.

# "College isn't the place to go for ideas."

Helen Keller, the author, activist and lecturer

## Why try to achieve success all alone?

Of course it's possible to achieve goals all on your own. Millions of people all over the world are striving to do just that right now. But it's tough, exhausting and takes time.

So why do so many people get caught in the trap of thinking that going solo is the best way? And why do so many people think that achieving anything significant must be tough and time-consuming?

Part of the answer is the belief that in order to achieve success in life you must do things which make you deserving. In other words, many people believe that success comes after you've first struggled and that the link between success and struggle is unavoidable. That's not entirely true because it does not necessarily follow that you first have to struggle on your own.

The fact is that all of us have strengths and weaknesses. For that reason we should enlist the help of others and, in turn, help them. When we do, the world – Mother Nature, the Universe, God or whatever you want to call the high-power – rewards us by making things easier and speedier to achieve.

## We all need support

Abraham Lincoln is an example of a great man who overcame problems with the help of others as is John D. Rockefeller. They each faced up to their weaknesses and enlisted the help of other people.

Henry Ford desperately wanted to succeed and he identified early on that he would need to gather people around him who were strong where he was weak. His dream was to bring the affordable cars to the masses and he knew there was no way he could do that alone given his weak points.

You become more effective when you focus and concentrate on improving your strengths whilst mitigating your weaknesses. Having areas for development is human and the important first step is to acknowledge that you have them as Ford did. The next step is to seek out other people to compensate for your weaknesses because everyone needs support in their lives.

Helen Keller became one of the world's most inspirational people with the help of a partner called Anne Sullivan who, amongst other things, acted as her eyes and ears.

However, in today's society we are generally not very practised at working in harmony and supporting each other unconditionally without any expectation of reward. Society and businesses tend to recognise and reward individual efforts and achievements rather than collective ones.

We're taught to try and fix our weaknesses instead of playing to our strengths and enlisting the help of others to make up for our shortcomings.

Many of us have been taught that going it alone and being self-sufficient are virtues and, up to a point, they are. Of course it is possible to achieve your dreams all on your own but this approach is very hard work and needlessly time-consuming.

# The answer you've been seeking

The great masters from the early part of the last century knew something very special. They knew that the best way of achieving anything worthwhile is to do so collaboratively involving employees, customers and partners and other business associates.

Whether they were aware of it consciously or not, these great men and women used a process which has been called Masterminding and has been defined as "two or more people working together in a spirit of harmony and cooperation towards the achievements of definite goals". Masterminding is as relevant today as it was in the days of Henry Ford and Thomas Edison.

Don't be fooled by the apparent simplicity of this technique based on its definition. It might seem too obvious and you might be thinking to yourself: "That's what I do anyway. I have people that support and help me."

But there is more to Masterminding than first appears apparent. It is a very focused and organised process and requires the adoption of a certain mindset and the application of particular skills and techniques. It does also require discipline and commitment but the rewards are huge.

Throughout history people have used Masterminding to achieve their goals and to solve problems. They may not have called it by the same name but if they got together to discuss their dreams and worked together in a spirit of harmony towards the achievement of those definite goals, then Masterminding is what they were doing.

"To listen closely and reply well is the highest perfection we are able to attain in the art of conversation."

Francois de La Rochefoucauld,
French author and nobleman.

The paybacks of Masterminding are many and varied. Here are just a few:

- Focus – Masterminding compels you to focus on your goals more frequently and hence you achieve them faster;

- Sharing and support – Masterminding makes you realise that other people are going through, or will have previously been through, the very same challenges you are experiencing. You will draw consolation from that and will gain from the experiences of others. Masterminding is a safe environment where you can share your dreams and problems and be supported;

- Inspiration and energy – you will be stimulated and motivated by other people.

A Masterminding group can help you to:

- set and achieve your goals;
- deliver on your commitments;
- overcome obstacles;
- develop belief in yourself;
- model the positive behaviours, habits and traits of other people.

You will be:

- listened to;
- supported and encouraged;
- held accountable;
- inspired by other people;
- able to bounce ideas off people and receive constructive feedback.

"The secret of my success is a two word answer: Know people."

Harvey S. Firestone

Over time, you will also develop profound and sustainable relationships with what will become your special group of people.

Masterminding enables you to model the traits and habits of successful people. People take on the nature, habits and the power of the thoughts of people with whom they associate.

Henry Ford added the power of the intelligence, experience, knowledge and spirits of the other great men in his Masterminding team of Edison, Burbank, Burroughs and Firestone to his own ability.

Masterminding also allows you to gain exposure to a wide source of ideas which helps to shorten the time it takes to get a project from concept to reality.

The aim of this book is to ignite your interest in Masterminding and to teach you how to do it for yourself. Once you have read the book, you will have the desire and the tools to go out and try Masterminding for yourself.

The truth is that people desperately need a different approach to solving problems and achieving success. Doing it alone is not the best way.

As Einstein said, "The significant problems we face cannot be solved at the same level of thinking we were at when we created them." Masterminding is the kind of advanced level thinking that allows for that to happen.

This powerful concept has helped millions of people over the years when nothing else had worked. If you use this technique there is no telling what you could achieve in your life and in your career or business.

If you commit to making this work and forming an effective Masterminding team, over time your fellow masterminders will become trusted confidants who you will rely on and turn to for priceless insights, candid feedback, valuable ideas, encouragement, inspiration and motivation.

If done properly, you can use Masterminding to achieve anything you want in life. This book will teach you how to Mastermind. You'll be shown how to form and run a highly performing Masterminding team for any purpose. Also you'll learn the mindset you'll need and the necessary skills and techniques that every member of the team will need to have.

Masterminding will become more and more used in the years to come and this thinking revolution will really take-off amongst people and organisations who think in a progressive way.

# WHAT IS MASTERMINDING?

To repeat again, Masterminding is when two or more people come together in a spirit of cooperation and harmony to achieve definite goals, be they shared ones or individual ambitions.

There are some key words in that definition. There is an old saying that two heads are better than one and that is so true. All of us have a limited amount of knowledge, skills and experiences to draw on which means that we need to team up with other people in order to get a job done.

How often do people come together in a true spirit of cooperation? Particularly in the business environment, most teams and departments don't work together, although they may claim that they do. They may give an appearance of working in harmony but very often individual or departmental agendas are being played out.

And finally, how often do you find teams working to very specific and definite goals that they're all agreed on? Often goals are vague or each person in the team has their own interpretation of what they are trying to achieve.

In contrast, the idea behind Masterminding is to amicably coordinate the combined mind power contained within the group in order to achieve precisely defined objectives.

It is important to be clear what Masterminding is not. It is not group mentoring and is not a form of life or business coaching, for example.

# "An idea is salvation by imagination."

Frank Lloyd Wright, one of the most
prominent and influential architects of the
first half of the 20th century

Coaching is a practice which has grown in popularity in recent years and typically involves a trained professional using mentoring, values assessment, behaviour modification, behaviour modelling and goal setting techniques to assist clients. Often a life coach is seeking to draw answers out of the client. Masterminding, on the other hand, harnesses the collective mind power of a group of people to produce extraordinary results for each member.

Many of the greatest human minds of all time have freely admitted that they did not originate the ideas that made them famous all on their own. Rather, they have likened what happened to tuning into a cosmic radio station and receiving the idea and inspiration from there.

The simple fact of the matter is that people who have used Masterminding have become great beyond their wildest dreams and those who have not have had a much harder time of it.

## Masterminding makes achieving what you want easier

Masterminding does not require you to work harder nor does it require a great amount of education. Through Masterminding you will learn how to relax confident in the knowledge that you can achieve your goals easily and speedily.

You will have fewer feelings of anxiety or fear when you are a member of a Masterminding group. You'll learn how to help other people identify their true desires and you will help them to achieve them.

"One plus one, doesn't equal two. It becomes the power of eleven."

Mark Victor Hansen, Creator of the *'Chicken Soup for the Soul'* franchise and the world's No.1 selling non-fiction author

The truth is that we've been making this thing called life too hard for too long. A myth needs to be exploded: the reason why so many people find it so hard to achieve their goals – be they be business or personal – is not because they're not trying hard enough. It's because they're trying to achieve success without the help and support of others.

Say you set out to try to build a business all on your own. Although it'll be a great adventure, it will also be tough, tremendously demanding in terms of time, money and energy plus it will be confusing, at times, and very often overwhelming. You'll feel alone and burdened most of the time.

You'll often feel a mix of excitement at the possibilities and the potential, but also you will feel weighed down with all the things you'll need to learn and all the things you'll need to do. Very often there won't be the time needed to go through the learning curve. Even if you have a business partner or coach you'll still end up having to figure out most things yourself.

One of the beauties of having a Masterminding team is that you won't have to keep reinventing the wheel to take your business to the next level.

What happens when people cooperate and synchronise in this way is that they soak up and amplify each others creative powers and result-achieving capabilities. When you blend mind power in this way, magic happens.

The human mind is a form of energy. When two or more minds 'mastermind', they form a great bank of energy, plus a third, invisible force which connects to the Infinite Intelligence of the Universe.

# There is nothing new about Masterminding

Whether utilised knowingly or not, almost all of the great accomplishments of history were achieved using this method. Since the beginning of time, probably, men and women have achieved great things when they've helped each other work towards definite objectives in a true spirit of harmony.

Examples of powerful masterminders include:

- Orville and Wilbur Wright working together to achieve what was considered the impossible by building the world's first aeroplane;

- Bill Gates and Paul Allen pooling their talents to create the most successful software company of all time, namely Microsoft;

- Andrew Carnegie pulling a team together that built the world's largest steel company.

Also the writer Dale Carnegie, who wrote the multimillion selling book *How to Win Friends and Influence People*, attributed his success entirely to Masterminding. The company he founded, Dale Carnegie Training, is now represented in 70 countries and has more than 2,700 instructors. Over the years, approximately 7 million people have completed Dale Carnegie Training courses.

A group that called themselves the Chicago 6 are another example of the power of Masterminding . They were a team of six businessmen who met every Saturday night at a restaurant during the early 1900s. When they started out none of them had any money but they all ultimately became millionaires. They'd probably be described as self-made millionaires but the truth is that they were mastermind-made millionaires.

# The origins of Masterminding

Although as a method, Masterminding has been used since the beginning of time probably, it was with the publication of the book *Think and Grow Rich* written by the Napoleon Hill in 1937 that the word Masterminding was first coined. It was in this book that Masterminding was first identified as a common trait amongst successful people also.

Napoleon Hill was one of the great thinkers of the early part of the last century and Andrew Carnegie was one of the great business people of that era.

From very humble beginnings Carnegie built a huge steel empire and it was he who commissioned Hill to write the historic book and gave him the task of interviewing the most successful business people in the world.

He asked Hill to find out what their lives were like, how they thought, what actions they took, and what their habits were. The search was on for patterns and common threads and the task led Hill into identifying and understanding the basic elements of success. In total it took him 29 years to write the book and in that time he conducted over 500 interviews.

"Create a definite plan for carrying out your desire and begin at once, whether you are ready or not to put this plan into action."

Napoleon Hill

Key amongst his findings was the discovery that every single one of these brilliant people relied on an inner circle of advisers and peers who collaborated on a regular basis. This team of people offered advice, help, motivation, encouragement and criticism. They inspired each other to do better. Hill said there is no substitute for the education, experience and influence and capital of other people.

In the book, Napoleon Hill also talked about the fact that power is essential for the accumulation of money because goals are lifeless unless you have the power to turn those plans into action. He said that power may be acquired through infinite intelligence (in other words, the intelligence of the universe), the experience of other people and research and experimentation. He said that individuals will encounter great difficulty acquiring the power that comes from this knowledge if they depend on their efforts alone.

Masterminding is not new. We've all heard about the legend of King Arthur and his Knights of the Round Table, but, what you may not have heard suggested is that this legendary figure was in many ways a pioneering Masterminder.

King Arthur's mission was to unify England and to promote peace and success. To do that, he assembled around him a group of the best and most well-mannered warriors in Europe.

He was determined to not make the same mistake as other Kings had made and took steps to prevent his team from becoming political, restless and power-crazy. He wanted them all to see themselves as equals with a voice that would be heard.

"Do the one thing you think you cannot do. Fail at it. Try again. Do better the second time. The only people who never tumble are those who never mount the high wire. This is your moment. Own it."

Oprah Winfrey

And, according to legend, that is exactly what happened. Supported by Merlin and his Knights of the Round Table, King Arthur ruled justly and fairly. He righted wrongs, he risked great dangers yet he remained dignified and possessed great courage and insight. And he was able to do that because of the Masterminding team he had around him.

The famous Round Table was significant too. It was both practical and symbolic. King Arthur dispensed with the traditional rectangular table favoured by other monarchs because he knew that if everyone sat around a round table then no position at the table would signify any greater importance than any other. He wanted his knights to talk to each other as equals.

Long, rectangular tables with the boss at the top inevitably create an uneasy atmosphere relating to status and pose practical problems of people, potentially, not being heard. Round or square tables do not present the same problem and make it easier to pool mental effort.

## The Science behind Masterminding

There is a scientific basis to Masterminding. It is about synergy which is defined as "the interaction of two or more agents or forces so that their combined effect is greater than the sum of their individual effects."

A healthy human body is an example of synergy at work because it is a harmonious interaction of subsystems organised in a way that is mutually supportive of the whole. The body organs support each other and human life.

"No two minds ever come
together without thereby creating
a third, invisible, intangible force which
may be likened to a third mind."

Napoleon Hill

In business the term synergy is often used to describe cooperative dealings among groups that create a superior result. Synergy is a win-win situation. However, it is a state of affairs often desired after, but rarely realised. The sum of the whole can be greater than the sum of its parts and two heads are better than one – provided, that is, certain rules are followed. It is not a given. You need harmony, for example, to be in place along with other factors which we will get into later in the book.

With Masterminding, you are using your thoughts to create a connection to the creative mechanism of other people's minds. And the collective energies of two or more minds working in accord with each other is many, times greater than the sum of the individual energies involved.

With Masterminding, you are combining your own creativity with that of others plus you are connecting with the power of Infinite Intelligence.

Another point to bear in mind is that in Masterminding you also draw on the strength of the minds of other people in the group. Other like-minded people can believe for you the things you may find difficult to believe for yourself.

In a sense Masterminding is a form of meditation because you are working in harmony with other people and thereby connecting with a higher level of intelligence.

"Infinite intelligence is the
source of all information: energy,
matter, and of course, also space and
time, the structure and the fabric
of the universe."

Deepak Chopra, Author and Speaker

## Masterminding is an advanced form of thinking

When you mastermind you, in effect, plug your brain into the brains of other people and in so doing solve problems that you'd never have solved by yourself.

There are essentially two characteristics of the Masterminding principle. One is easy to understand but the second is more difficult.

The first is more obvious and tangible, because it is easy to see the advantages you would gain by being in a cooperative alliance with other like-minded people who offer you their advice, ideas and support.

The second characteristic is almost supernatural and spiritual in nature so is more difficult to appreciate and see. In Napoleon Hill's own words: "No two minds ever come together without, thereby, creating a third invisible, intangible force which may be likened to a third mind."

This 'third mind' is, in effect, what we previously called Infinite Intelligence. It is the collective brainpower of the world in which we live.

You will experience this 'third mind' when you are part of a highly performing Masterminding group. As an example, ideas and thoughts will just pop into your head and you will think: "Where did that come from? I've never had that thought before and yet the words came out of my mouth!"

To explain the advanced form of thinking which Masterminding represents, Napoleon Hill drew an analogy between the functioning of the human brain and batteries. He said that a group of brains connected and coordinated in a spirit of harmony will create more thought energy than a single brain operating alone, just as a group of electric batteries will provide more energy than a single battery.

You see this phenomenon in Nature. For example, if you bring the flames of two candles together they don't create twice the amount of light, but four times the quantity. The effect is exponential.

The increased mindpower energy created by a Masterminding group is available to each and every one of the members of that group. So when a group is united the flow of ideas is extraordinary.

When you use Masterminding you think bigger and think faster. Combining the power of several minds to solve problems, provide advice, offer different perspectives and achieve goals means that greater results are created than ever would be the case by going it alone.

So Masterminding is about leverage. It is about leveraging the abilities of the other people in the group but also leveraging the greatest store of power that exists, namely, Infinite Intelligence. Masterminding provides you with positional advantage and the power to act effectively.

Masterminding is a support system of like-minded people. For it to work in an optimum way everyone has to benefit and everyone has to contribute. Masterminding can make a winner out of the loser in a shorter timeframe than any other technique you will come across. Masterminding is the result of positive minds working together and helping each other.

## Great masterminders

One of the most famous examples of the power of Masterminding is the group mentioned previously, namely the Chicago 6. Two of the more famous members were William Wrigley – he of Wrigley's chewing gum fame – and John D Hertz.

When they formed in the early 1900s, this group of half a dozen men were all virtually penniless. They met for dinner every

Saturday at a local Chicago restaurant. They discussed their objectives for their businesses and gave and received help in many forms. And after just a few years each one was worth several millions of dollars. They started their successful businesses with a great deal of help from their Masterminding Group and their stories are truly inspirational.

William Wrigley, for example, overcame near bankruptcy on several occasions and was a pioneer in many ways. He was born in Philadelphia and he moved to Chicago and founded the William Wrigley, Jr. Company in 1891.

He blazed a trail by taking advantage of advertising methods that were rarely used in his time such as print media, plus he was one of the first manufacturers to place products available for sale next to cash registers. Today, the company he founded dominates the market, with almost half the chewing gum sales in the United States.

"If I could solve all the
problems myself, I would."

Thomas A. Edison

John D Hertz is another example of huge achievement from humble beginnings. He was born in Austria but emigrated to Chicago. He founded the Yellow Cab Company and the Chicago Motor Coach Company. Hertz ran the taxicab company until 1929, when he left to found another rental car company, Hertz Rent-a-Car which has since grown to 6,500 locations with a fleet of over half a million vehicles.

If the Chicago 6 could use Masterminding to make millions then so can you use the method to achieve whatever you want – be it financial or otherwise. Masterminding is how you'll make good things happen in your life.

The scientist, inventor, statesman, philosopher, musician and economist Benjamin Franklin also masterminded. He's famous these days as one of America's Founding Fathers and is regarded as one of that country's greatest ever citizens, but what is less well known is that he ran a Friday evening Masterminding club, called Junto, for many years.

It started in 1727 when he persuaded 12 of his friends to form an alliance committed to shared improvement. The group lasted for 40 years and ultimately became the core of the American Philosophical Society.

One of the things they did was to dream up publicly beneficial ideas. Projects they brought to fruition include the first library in the USA, volunteer fire departments, the first public hospital, police departments, paved streets and the University of Pennsylvania. At Junto meetings, members suggested books, businesses, and friends to each other.

"Early to bed and early
to rise makes a man healthy,
wealthy, and wise."

Benjamin Franklin

One of the principles of Junto was that club members were prohibited from saying anything that indicated they had a fixed opinion on a subject. This is because they believed that you do not know it all and need to be open to other views and ideas. This point is best illustrated via an analogy...

> ... For a man travelling through foggy weather, people in the distance in all directions appear enveloped in fog whilst those who are near to him appear clear. The truth is, though, that these people are as much in the fog as those in the distance, but that is not how it seems.

So to be wise, you need to be aware that you too are in the fog. There are many options and many truths out there. So the more eyes we can see with and the more people we can listen to, the wiser we become.

One of the greatest of all Masterminding alliances was that between Thomas Edison, Henry Ford, Harvey Firestone, the naturalist John Burroughs and the botanist Luther Burbank. They believed in their dreams and drove each other forward. Thomas Edison's prolific inventiveness owed a lot to the work he did in working in harmony with fellow Masterminders.

Henry Ford relied on this Masterminding group to achieve his dreams. They were Thomas Edison, Harvey Firestone, John Burroughs and Luther Burbank and they called themselves The Vagabonds.

They were unlikely friends in many ways. Edison, Ford and Firestone were driven business people but John Burroughs was a famous author and naturalist whilst Luther Burbank was a scientist and botanist and developed over 800 strains and varieties of plants. They all shared something in common, though: they shared a sense of wonder, curiosity and the spirit of innovation.

"Be a good listener. Your ears will never get you in trouble."

Frank Tyger

They supported each other and, significantly, were the driving force that made each other accountable to make their dreams a reality.

Ford said this of his first meeting with Edison:

> **"No man up to then had given me any encouragement. I had hoped that I was headed right. Sometimes I knew that I was, sometimes I only wondered, but here, all at once and out of a clear sky, the greatest inventive genius in the world (Edison) had given me complete approval. The man who knew most about electricity in the world had said that for the purpose, my gas motor was better than any electric motor could be."**

Such an impact did his Masterminding group have on him that Henry Ford built tributes to his friends.

For example:

- he had his estate's designer build a wildlife grotto made of rocks from John Burroughs' boyhood home

- the Field Room at his Fair Lane estate contained wood carvings of each of the Vagabonds

- the Garden Office of Luther Burbank is at the Henry Ford Museum's Greenfield Village

"Genius is 1% inspiration,
99% perspiration."

Thomas A. Edison

Dale Carnegie was a lecturer, author, and pioneer in the field of public speaking and the psychology of the successful personality. He said that he owed everything he ever achieved to Masterminding.

Born into poverty in Missouri, at high school and college he was active in debating clubs. When he graduated he became a salesman and an actor. Eventually he went on to teach public speaking. He became an instant success with the hugely popular book *How to Win Friends and Influence People*.

The tycoon Andrew Carnegie had a personal Masterminding group of 20 experts and they worked together to create the world's greatest steel empire. From a very poor background in Scotland, Andrew Carnegie's family emigrated to America. Carnegie was absolutely determined to escape poverty and went onto become the richest man in the world. After building his fortune with the help of others, Carnegie then gave away millions.

There are some modern-day examples of masterminders too. Bill Gates, the richest man of this century for example, and Paul Allen pooled their collective brainpower to build the world's largest software company on the back of Masterminding principles.

Also, for many years Michael Eisner, the ex-CEO of Disney, convened a mastermind meeting of elite CEOs in Sun Valley, Idaho. Donald Trump also understands the power of many minds and has regularly brought together CEOs to leverage each other's success. Experience comes in two flavours, he says, yours and other peoples. It is foolish to ignore the experience of others.

"Opportunity is missed by
most people because it is dressed in
overalls and looks like work."

Thomas A. Edison

# Types of Masterminding

Many types of Masterminding groups are possible. You can have a career or business Masterminding group to help you progress and you can have a personal Masterminding group to help you with your health and fitness, family relationship, financial, lifestyle, and spiritual goals.

There are different types of business Masterminding group in operation. For example, in the USA there are groups such as the Young Presidents Organisation, the Executive Committee and CEO Clubs.

You can have Masterminding groups within large organisations focused on delivering specific outcomes that pull in expertise from different departments and different locations. You can have Masterminding groups that are industry-specific or ones that are multi-industry.

In the home-based or small business setting, a Masterminding group can act as an experienced board of directors or team of advisers you don't have to pay a salary or fee to.

In business, it does help if members are from non-competing areas as occasions will arise when people will want to discuss sensitive information in a safe and confidential environment.

Masterminders may want to do business with each other but in many ways it is best to keep business separate just in case something occurs which could damage relationships.

"You can make more friends
in two months by becoming interested
in other people than you can in two
years by trying to get other people
interested in you."

Dale Carnegie

Another type of Masterminding is what you could call internal or virtual Masterminding. This requires a great deal of imagination and belief in the process but anyone can do it.

What you do is to create an imaginary Masterminding group composed of the greatest people you know. They might be heroes of yours, and it doesn't matter if they are living or dead.

The idea is to have imaginary meetings with these people in your mind. Set aside some time, relax and have an imaginary Masterminding get-together with your virtual team. Create a picture in your mind of them arriving at your meeting. Ask them questions and make note of their answers.

At first, this may seem like fantasy but stick with it because in time you will find that your brain actually tunes into the brains and energies of these people. Virtual Masterminding works.

## What Masterminding can deliver

With Masterminding, it's possible to achieve more in a year than you could do in a decade by working alone because you have more power available to you. Remember, Masterminding employs the power of synergy: one plus one does not equal two, it equals three or more.

Masterminding is the power of collective wisdom and can deliver exponential and immediate results.

Masterminding is the easiest way to breathe new life and activity into any situation in your life, career or business.

The insights, connections and opportunities you get when you mastermind can save you an inordinate amount of time and money. Masterminding is exhilarating and profoundly impactful.

"Small opportunities are often
the beginning of great enterprises."

Demosthenes

Masterminding can be a sounding board where you can seek feedback on where you are at or on new ideas or plans you have. You will learn about new concepts and you will set your business goals higher than you would have done previously. You will learn through the mistakes and experiences of other people. You will be held accountable and, in turn, you will hold other people accountable for achieving what they say they want to achieve.

It takes you out of your comfort zone when necessary and helps you to overcome your fears. Masterminding can be your safety net because your Masterminding group will be seeking to make sure that you do not fall and, if you do, they will pick you up again.

You will regularly surprise yourself at the things that you say and that other people come up with in Masterminding meetings. When a Masterminding session is working in an optimum way you will open yourselves up to a source of power that will amaze you.

Because you make Masterminding meetings a regular part of your life the results you get stack on each other. In monetary terms, Masterminding is like compound interest because of the pace of progress you can make.

"We make a living by what we get; we make a life by what we give."

Sir Winston Churchill

Magic happens at Masterminding meetings. Whatever outcomes you are striving for, you can count on getting the necessary solutions, ideas, previous experiences, plans and contacts that will get you closer to where you want to go to.

Masterminding is energising, provides motivation and offers accountability. You get access to resources you would not have previously known about and you get connections and contacts you would never have dreamed possible. You get to hear about the experiences and the lessons learned by other people, thereby saving you the trouble, cost and heartache of making the same mistakes yourself.

Masterminding is a technique which can be applied in any area. For example, it can help with your marriage. It can help you find a marriage partner. It can help your creativity and it can help your bottom line if you're in business.

In the business environment, Masterminding can enable you to increase your revenues, increase your market share, bring down your costs, increase your margins, and improve customer service at a much faster pace than you would otherwise be able to do. It can bring you increased productivity and income along with ways to work smarter and not harder with the help of other people.

When part of a Masterminding group, you have other people focusing their undivided attention on you and helping you. It enables you to make informed decisions on such things as marketing, planning financing and technical issues.

"The spirit in which a thing is given
determines that in which the debt
is acknowledged; it's the intention, not the
face-value of the gift, that's weighed."

Seneca

## The factors that make Masterminding work

Masterminding works best when certain features are in place. A particular attitude of mind is required of participants, for example. It requires people to have an understanding of what they know and, just as importantly, what they don't know. They need to be open to suggestions and the help of other people. Masterminding involves committing to regularly turn up and help to contribute to the success of other people.

When Masterminding groups fail, it is normally because of one or more of the following reasons.

People:

- being fearful of sharing their problems or goals;
- being afraid of looking inadequate in some way;
- believing that they can solve all their problems themselves;
- not fully understanding the value of a Masterminding group and not having the patience to wait for the results to come;
- thinking they have nothing to give;
- being afraid of other people stealing their ideas;
- not feeling worthy of being helped.

The best results are normally achieved when a Masterminding group is led by a facilitator. This takes away the possibility of the agenda being overtly or subconsciously lead by a member of the group. It also enables members to fully participate in a meeting without having to think about group management or leadership issues. The facilitator needs to understand group dynamics and the Masterminding principle.

"If you're going to be thinking,
you may as well think big."

Donald Trump

Masterminding groups succeed when members share a particular mindset and believe that the knowledge, experience, information and wisdom and perspective of other people are important things and that to succeed long-term you need an endless and ongoing supply of them.

Masterminding works best where:

- Groups consist of no more than 10 members. 6 to 8 is the ideal for reasons of team dynamics. Too many members can make for very long meetings;
- Members are not close friends or family members. You will develop a close bond with your fellow Masterminders and will care for them but it does not necessarily follow that you need to have been or will become close friends with everyone in order for Masterminding to work effectively;
- There is a mix of people from different backgrounds and disciplines with a varied mix of life experiences.

Other critical success factors are:

- Sticking to the system and the process;
- Having a diversity of people and opinions in the group;
- There being a focus within the group on achieving specific objectives;
- People believing that every meeting is important;
- Everyone giving and everyone getting something back in return;
- People being held to high standards and demanding the best of themselves.

"Lack of money is no obstacle.
Lack of an idea is an obstacle."

Ken Hakuta, TV presenter

# THE MASTERMINDING MINDSET

For Masterminding to be successful a particular attitude of mind is required by the people involved.

Masterminders need to:
- be prepared to dream in an unlimited way;
- be prepared to ask for their dreams to come true;
- possess a burning desire;
- believe that there is a solution to every problem;
- welcome the fact that they have more power than they realise;
- believe in the power of teamwork;
- believe in sharing.

Let's explore this mindset now.

## Unlimited dreaming

Masterminding requires that you are very vigorous in your thinking about what you want to create. You need to believe that anything you desire can be achieved and you need to have a very clear vision of what that dream looks like for you.

This is not a new idea of course because over the years so many successful business and political leaders have spoken about the importance of having a seemingly impossible and compelling vision, but rarely do individuals take heed of this advice in their own lives.

In his book *Think and Grow Rich* Napoleon Hill said: "One must realize that all who have accumulated great fortunes first did a certain amount of dreaming, hoping, wishing, desiring, and planning before they acquired money."

However, in today's society we are also not very practised at dreaming, discovering and going after our true desires. This means that rarely do we listen to what you could call our soul, which is the part of us that knows what we really want in life. It speaks quietly and can be difficult to hear above the noise of everyday life.

The Latin meaning of the word desire is 'of the Father' and what that means in this context is that you are capable of having what you truly desire.

So you need to dream in an unlimited way so as to create your vision. You need to engage the creative part of your brain. You need to take off the shackles and get out of the box. You need to get yourself out of caged-in thinking and you do that by tapping into your creative soul.

Part of that limited box thinking is the belief that things have to be hard, difficult and painstaking. We see problems as bigger than they really are because that's what we look for. We spend too much time thinking about the problem and not enough time thinking about what a solution could look like.

There is plenty of time for the logical and realistic brain to do its work and that time comes later on once the dream is built. You first need to access the creative territory of your mind.

Psychologists call the limitations we put on ourselves 'premature cognitive commitments'. These represent the box within which we think and therefore the way in which we live our lives.

We get into a comfort zone and this is not always a good thing and, what happens is that unless something very disruptive happens to us such as a terrible event, we tend to tolerate a slow and steady increase in pain caused by the limited box. The effect of the box is numbing rather than alarming.

Let's look at a real-life example of this: Global Warming is the gradual increase in global temperatures caused by the emission of gases that trap the sun's heat in the Earth's atmosphere. It is thought to be responsible for some of the changes in global climate patterns that we're seeing right now, but because the changes are, by and large, slow and gradual they aren't noticed as much as they ought to be.

The way the limited box works is subtle and affects all areas of our lives including the goals we set ourselves. If our limited box doesn't think something is possible it tends to edit out opposing evidence and lets in data that reinforces that view. What we consider possible for ourselves is merely a reflection of our premature cognitive commitments. We get ourselves committed to a particular view of reality.

But the great news is that the human mind is geared towards creating. It doesn't have to think in a limited way, even though it may have been habitualised into being that way. It loves dreaming and creating a vision.

"The reason most people never reach their goals is that they don't define them, or ever seriously consider them as believable or achievable. Winners can tell you where they are going, what they plan to do along the way, and who will be sharing the adventure with them."

Denis Watley, Author and Speaker

Imagination is one of the capabilities we have all been born with but you must give it the freedom it needs. With your imagination you can create your future. You are not limited to the circumstances that you find yourself in right now. And neither is anyone else.

Also, the Masterminding process overrides any feelings of limitation. You achieve without getting exhausted in the process as too often happens when you try to achieve goals all on your own. The good news is that as you go after your dream you don't have to figure out the solutions all by yourself if you have Masterminding partners to help you.

## Ask and you shall receive

Masterminders need to ask for what they want and decide to go after their dreams and goals no matter what.

It's no good just thinking about your goals. Writing down your goals is a form of asking. As is praying for what you want.

No matter how large and seemingly unrealistic your goals are, you also need to share your goals with people that you can trust. You should not tell people about your goals who will mock and ridicule them.

Your goals at this stage are fragile and need protecting. You should tell your Masterminding group about your goals as they are there to encourage and believe in you.

"Until one is committed, there is
hesitancy, the chance to draw back —
Concerning all acts of initiative
(and creation), there is one elementary
truth that ignorance of which kills
countless ideas and splendid plans: that
the moment one definitely commits
oneself, then Providence moves too.
All sorts of things occur to help
one that would never otherwise have
occurred. A whole stream of events issues
from the decision, raising in one's favour
all manner of unforeseen incidents and
meetings and material assistance, which
no man could have dreamed would have
come his way. Whatever you can do, or
dream you can do, begin it.
Boldness has genius, power, and
magic in it. Begin it now."

Goethe

# A burning desire

Possessing a passion to achieve a goal feels good. With it, you are confident that you can realize what you have set out to achieve and you know the 'how' will show up when you need it to.

Burning desire is not about manic activity, as some people think. Manic activity is normally driven by panic and fear.

Desire is not an excessive or compulsive state of mind either. It is not about overactivity because that leads to a rollercoaster ride of crash and burn. Up one minute, down the next.

To achieve a burning desire you must practice feeling desire on a consistent basis. Achieving big goals is more like a marathon than a sprint and you need the fuel to get there. Desire provides that energy and creates resolve, which means cutting off all possibilities of failure in your mind.

Desire also leads to faith, which is a state of mind where you are sure something will work out the way you want it to even if current circumstances do not suggest that is possible.

When you turn on your desire, your mind becomes like a finely tuned laser. This is how you overcome adversity – you turn up your desire for what you want.

"Only passions, great passions,
can elevate the soul to
great things."

Denis Diderot, French Philosopher and Writer

## There is a solution to every problem

"Well, what use is dreaming and deciding if I don't know how to make that vision a reality?" you might then say. Well the other part of the good news is that your mind is a highly tuned goal seeking and problem solving mechanism.

Like an aeroplane, it can take you from where you are now to the target you set for yourself, adjusting along the way to keep you on course and overcoming obstacles. Again like an aeroplane, your brain has the equivalent of a navigation system that makes these kinds of adjustments. And the role of your Masterminding group is to service, maintain and fine tune your target-seeking system.

How many people have you ever met who believed that they could achieve whatever they really wanted but never did anything about it? Why is that?

How is it you can believe that you can achieve anything but never get into action? The most probable answer is that these people believe it will be too difficult with too many problems to solve, too time-consuming and too exhausting. They find it difficult to muster up the energy, drive and willpower and end up getting caught up in day-to-day life and saying, "I'll do it tomorrow".

That doesn't have to be you. Examine any person who has acquired a fortune or wealth of any kind and you'll find that they either consciously or unconsciously used the Masterminding concept.

"Nothing in the world can take the place of Persistence. Talent will not; nothing is more common than unsuccessful men with talent. Genius will not; unrewarded genius is almost a proverb. Education will not; the world is full of educated derelicts. Persistence and determination alone are omnipotent. The slogan 'Press On' has solved and always will solve the problems of the human race."

Calvin Coolidge, 30th President of the United States

## Don't be afraid of your power

There is tremendous power when two or more people make a strong decision to do something. A strong agreement between two or more has more power than a shallow agreement between thousands of people. Don't underestimate the power that you can unleash when you reach a strong agreement on something.

You truly can pull up trees but you have to be willing to unleash your greatness and that can be a bit scary for some people.

So are you willing to unleash your greatness? True power is not about overpowering people or diminishing them in some way. It is not about being better than they are and seeing yourself as superior. Greatness is about charm, generosity, friendliness and genuineness.

However, no matter how much power you possess through Masterminding, at times, you will feel in need of help. There is nothing wrong with being in need. It doesn't mean that you are weak. It simply means that you are human. Some people think needing help means that they are weak. It simply means they are human and need help and support.

## Teamwork

We are all amazing but when we team up with others we are more than we ever could be by working alone. Ultimately, your greatness is going to come down to whether you become part of a great team or not. Because we all have strengths and weaknesses, we need others to bring out our full talents, results and abilities.

"Our deepest fear is not that we are inadequate. Our deepest fear is that we are powerful beyond measure. It is our light, not our darkness that most frightens us. We ask ourselves: "Who am I to be brilliant, gorgeous, talented, and fabulous?" Actually, who are you not to be? You are a child of God. Your playing small does not serve the world. There is nothing enlightened about shrinking so that other people won't feel insecure around you. We are all meant to shine, as children do. We were born to make manifest the glory of God that is within us. It is not just in some of us; it is in everyone. And as we let our own light shine, we unconsciously give other people permission to do the same. As we are liberated from our own fear, our presence automatically liberates others."

Marianne Williamson, Author and Spiritual Activist

A team can be defined as a group of people working interdependently.

An exercise which is often done by trainers to illustrate the power of teamwork is to give a really tough puzzle to a group and to ask each person to work separately on coming up with the answer. At the end of the allotted time, the trainer asks how many people have solved the puzzle. Typically no hands are raised, but when the whole group is asked to work on the puzzle together it is normally solved in no time at all. This is because they start talking and sharing ideas. So when a group works together in a cooperative way towards a definite aim, the problem is solved.

The right Masterminding team can provide you with the power, creativity, intuition you need to succeed at anything.

A good mix of people means that you will have others who are strong where you are weak.

Who you associate with goes a long way towards determining the kind of person you will become. You can take on the intelligence, experience, knowledge and spiritual forces of the people you associate with.

## Sharing

Sharing is giving and receiving. It is one of Nature's laws because the world operates through a process of dynamic exchange. Things don't work as they should if this law is flouted. For there to be a healthy balance in the Universe there needs to be an equal amount of giving and receiving.

"I believe that one of
life's greatest risks is never
daring to risk."

Oprah Winfrey

We're here to share. We're all part of Nature and we affect the balance of things if we just take and take or just give and give and are not prepared to receive.

Sharing is at the core of what Masterminding is all about so it's worth spending some time talking about sharing in a number of its aspects.

Firstly, it's important to understand that sharing is a two-way process. Giving and receiving are equally important. Some people think that, of the two, giving is the most difficult thing to do. However, in our hearts we all know that giving is not very difficult. When we think about when we have been most happy, it was probably when we were giving to others.

If you carry a sharing attitude around with you at all times, then giving and receiving become second nature. You can always help more than you do now. You can always receive more than you do now.

Always be open to sharing. People in need of help will come to you, from both within and from outside of your Masterminding group. For example, Calcutta was a gift to Mother Teresa. The opportunity to give on a massive scale came to her without her seeking it. She used to say: "I'm here to help and not to worry about where the money comes from."

The second important point about sharing is that you should share unconditionally. Sharing is not true sharing if you give 'with strings attached' or with the expectation or demand of receiving something in return.

"You must give some time to
your fellow men. Even if it's a little thing,
do something for others – something for
which you get no pay but the privilege
of doing it."

Albert Schweitzer, German theologian,
musician, philosopher and physician

For some people 'unconditionally' is a difficult word. If you give with conditions you will not enjoy the giving so much. True sharing means losing any desire to identify yourself with what you give.

The third key learning point about sharing is that you should not be discriminating about who you help. We are all one people and one universe. If you understand that you will feel safe as there is nothing to lose by giving.

A sharing attitude is a hugely beautiful quality in a person. Think about this for a second – what makes Nelson Mandela so attractive as a person? One of the reasons is because he shares unconditionally.

Great people are sharing people and their give and receive attitude contributes to the success they enjoy in life. Mahatma Gandhi and Bill Gates are two other examples of sharing people as is the investor Warren Buffett who in 2006 announced plans to donate $40 billion of his own money to good causes.

A sharing attitude to life enables you to overcome challenges also. For example, Gandhi said in his biography that he confronted ego all the time and yet he overcame it largely because his life was about sharing. He carried around with him a sharing template so that he shared even when he met with narrow-mindedness. What he was saying was that he broke down the bigotry and intolerance of other people with his sharing.

So sharing is the essence of life itself and once you start to share unconditionally then all you'll ever want to do is to share. You'll become addicted and sharing will be way you will live your life. The benefits of this will be outstanding and, manytimes, unexpected.

"You create your opportunities
by asking for them."

Patty Hansen, co-author
of *'Chicken Soup for the Kid's Soul'*

# HOW TO MASTERMIND

As you've read this far, you'll no doubt now want to know how to do Masterminding.

Masterminding consists of teams of people having regular face-to-face meetings where team members request and receive help from each other in relation to the goals they are going after and the problems and challenges they are meeting along the way.

Obviously your first job is to form your Masterminding team and you may want to have one or more groups – perhaps one for your career or business goals and one for your other life goals.

Whatever works for you is fine but it's important that the composition of your group is right, whichever approach you take.

## Finding people to be in your Masterminding group

An ideal group size is 6 to 8 people, so you might need to draw up a list of a dozen possible team members so that you can whittle it down.

Start by creating a list of the ideal characteristics and traits you are looking for in your Masterminding partners. For example, amongst your ideal team:

- What sort of experience do you want to have?
- What knowledge do you want to have?
- What skills do you want to have?

"Perpetual optimism is
a force multiplier."

Colin Powell

Remember as you draw up this wish list that there is value in difference and diversity. Do not pre-judge.

Once you've got your list there are many ways of finding people who are potentially suitable. While its best not to have close friends or family members in your group, it is a good idea to ask them if there is anyone they know who matches the profile of people you are looking for.

Your network of business associates is a good place to start your search. If you need to search further from home you could:

- post messages on Internet message boards;
- run classified advertisements on websites, newspapers and magazines;
- contact local trade associations and Chambers of Commerce;
- attend events of all kinds like seminars, workshops and talks;
- contact professional associations, community organisations and networking groups.

When you've got a list of possibles call them up, explain your idea and pitch them with your proposal.

## Selecting your team

Having got together a list of possible members who are interested in joining your Masterminding group, you'll want to go through a selection process. There'll no doubt be some people you know and some you don't know that well on your list. Choose the people carefully because the people you associate with are very important. They will influence you consciously and unconsciously.

# "A goal without a plan is just a wish."

Antoine de Saint-Exupery,
French Writer and Aviator

There are many factors you should weigh up and you'll want to spend up to an hour talking to each potential member so that you can make a thorough assessment of their suitability.

First and foremost, you should want people who have similar values and aspirations. Plus, you need people who can believe in the power of Masterminding. You need people who have a certain degree of belief in the process.

You'll also want to include people in your team who:

- are seeking personal growth;
- are goal orientated;
- think big;
- are positive;
- are team players;
- are trustworthy and who you can respect;
- understand and appreciate the value that Masterminding can bring;
- believe in you and the idea;
- are committed to getting results;
- have varied backgrounds and areas of expertise.

You should go for people who have a real desire to win in a collaborative way. You want people who want to do better, to be useful and to help others. Also you want people who respond well to, and act on, feedback.

"People's lives are a direct reflection
of the expectations of their peer group."

Tony Robbins, Author and Motivational Speaker

You want people who have a 'give rather than a get' mentality. People who just want to get will kill the energy of a Masterminding meeting. One of the problems in today's society it seems is that having an attitude which is not 'what's in it for me' is almost foreign to many people. You have to give before you get. This is a law of nature. You can't get the harvest until you've first planted the seeds and tended to your crop. You need a strong commitment from people. You want people to stick with it because the results can be just around the corner. You don't want quitters.

A key is that members must be willing to take on the help offered by other people. They shouldn't be too precious. You want people who are flexible and able to change direction and their approach, if necessary. Trust and integrity are also crucial.

Finally, you should seek a varied mix of mind power. Diversity is very important so go for a mix of ages, genders and ethnicity and if you are setting up a business Masterminding group, ideally, you should look for people from different industries.

Once you've selected your team, contact everyone to let them know the outcome. Issue a welcome letter to your team members and tell them that you will be in touch shortly with details of how they should prepare.

## Getting ready to launch your Masterminding team

The most important step in forming a successful Masterminding group is planning. As the founder of the group you need to take the initiative and make decisions. The decisions you make may not be perfect for everyone but you need to make a start as the details can be fine-tuned once your group is up and running.

There are a number of tasks you will need to carry out before you have your first meeting. First of all consider drawing up a Confidentiality Agreement. A signed agreement essentially serves as a pledge by the members of your team that any information shared will be not to be disclosed outside of the group unless consent is given.

If you decide that you want one, contact a solicitor to have one drafted and issue it to everyone beforehand (or visit www.masterminding.net/resources.htm). Ask them to read it and to ask any questions about it before your first meeting as you will want it signed by everyone as a first task.

You need to communicate the Masterminding groundrules to your group. The groundrules will ensure that all your meetings will run in accordance with Masterminding principles and they are detailed later in this chapter. You need to get your Masterminding team to sign up to adhering by them at all times.

You also need to think about a suitable venue, check on the availability of your team members and, from that, set a date and time for your first meeting. A good way of obtaining availability information is to ask for dates when people definitely cannot attend a meeting.

Your aim should be for your venue for Masterminding meetings to be within an hour's travelling distance of everyone. It's best if you sort out the first venue and your group decides on an appropriate venue for future meetings. A suggestion is that you opt for a hotel or a similar type of venue with a reasonably spacious and quiet lounge area which is conveniently located for all members of your group.

The ideal is that you agree a fixed date and time (for example, the first Tuesday evening of every month) so that people can plan ahead. Obviously, everyone will not be able to make every meeting but you should choose a schedule that ordinarily every member would be able to make.

The frequency of your meetings depends on the nature of the goals people are working on and how quickly they want to move.

Some Masterminding groups meet twice a week, some once a week, others once a month. It really depends on the goals being worked on and how fast you want to move. Some Masterminding groups meet just once or a couple of times a year but when they do meet they devote a whole day or even a weekend to Masterminding.

The important thing is that the meetings continue to happen and are run in an effective way.

One thing to bear in mind, however, is that it's a good idea that your first 5 or 6 meetings are held every two weeks, if not weekly. This is so that, as a group, you get to a stage of high performance sooner rather than later. After that you may decide to switch to meeting less often.

Give 3 to 4 weeks notice to your team of the first meeting. This is partly because you need to get your team to do some serious advance thinking about what they want to achieve through Masterminding.

# The Groundrules of Masterminding

For your Masterminding team to work most effectively and for everyone to be powered towards achieving their goals faster, the whole team must sign up to adhere to this set of groundrules.

### Seek harmony and rapport

Harmony is defined as 'compatibility in opinion and action' and rapport is a 'sense of mutual understanding and sympathy'. A spirit of harmony and rapport is essential for the effective running of a Masterminding session. Members need to work as one to help each other.

Tension or strife during a Masterminding session means creativity will not be sparked and the third force – Infinite Intelligence, in other words – will not be accessed. Complaining or whining, arguing with or negating other ideas is not productive. If negativity arises there's a need for a gentle reminder to people that they should express positive solutions.

When rapport and harmony is established between minds, ideas flow.

### Listen and ask good questions

Everyone must listen very carefully to hear the specific needs of the person who is talking. They mustn't just assume they know what the person talking is going through.

Masterminders must give their full attention so that they can provide insightful responses to what is being said. They should also watch for non-verbal communications such as facial expression, body language, tone of voice and expressions of emotion.

Sometimes listening so as to help people come up with their own solutions works very well because deep down people often know what to do and just need the answer drawing out of them through good listening.

## Display trust and keep discussions confidential

You must feel you can rely on the integrity and character of the people in your group. You won't feel you can be 100% open and honest in what you say unless you consider your fellow Masterminders are dependable. The best way to earn trust is to be trustworthy – if you prove you can be trusted then others are more likely to be trustworthy themselves.

Trust is important and that cannot be earned by fine words alone. It's what you do that matters. It's about keeping your word. It's about doing what you say you will and it's about relationships. Relationships are the cornerstone of any successful endeavour.

## Show respect and be honest

It is important that you appreciate and have consideration for the members of your group. Respect differences, be sincere and be truthful.

"You may be deceived if you trust too much, but you will live in torment if you do not trust enough."

Frank Crane, Presbyterian minister and Speaker

## Have faith and follow the system

It is crucial that everyone has belief in the Masterminding process and believes in the ability of their Masterminders to achieve their goals.

If you entertain doubts then Masterminding will not work for you at the level it should. The key is to work the system by following the plan set out in this book because it has been proven to work in the past for others and it can work for you too.

Also, believe in your fellow Masterminders because doing that can see them through when they themselves are doubtful.

## Show commitment

People must make and keep the pledges they make to the group. Members of the group will begin to rely on each other so people mustn't let each other down.

If someone fails to turn up for a meeting then it is not just they who will miss out, it is the other members because they will not get the benefit of the missing person's contributions. Punctuality and general reliability are extremely important.

## Be patient as the group could take time to develop

Be aware that people need to become familiar with the concept of Masterminding initially. They also need to get to know each other and what they're trying to achieve. People need to talk about and agree expectations and on how things will work.

"Men are born to
succeed, not fail."

Henry David Thoreau,
American Author and Philosopher

### Set clear individual and group goals

You cannot achieve anything unless you first define precisely what you're shooting for. So very early on, each member should define their goals and share them with the group. The group may decide that they want to aim for something as a group and this goal should be clearly defined also.

### Be positive and constructive

The job of any Masterminder is to always seek to help their fellow Masterminders to improve and make progress in their lives.

In this world we're surrounded by negativity and your Masterminding group needs to be a haven from that. This doesn't mean people should never criticise or make a judgement but it does mean that they should do so in a constructive way.

A major strength of Masterminding is that it results in a blending of the minds of all members. Jealousy, negativity, envy, friction and lack of interest on the part of any member will bring progress to a halt so should be dealt with straightaway.

## Your first Masterminding meeting

One of the challenges you may face is arranging your very first meeting. Unless they are in the same room together finding a day and time for 6 to 10 people to meet for the first time can be a challenge.

The ideal is obviously for every person to be present at the first meeting but if that proves impractical, do not worry – just opt for the day and time when most people can make it. The key is to just start.

Issue a formal invitation letter with details of the date, time and venue of the meeting. Include details and a brief biography of the other team members. In the letter enclose:

- a copy of the confidentiality agreement
- a copy of the Masterminding groundrules

Also remind team members to bring plenty of business cards and their contact list in whatever form that takes (this is something they will need to bring to every Masterminding meeting). Tell them that they should prepare a short biography of themselves to read out at meeting 1.

The first meeting will mainly be a 'getting to know you' session where everyone introduces themselves and gives the group an insight into the goals and challenges they want the team to help them with in the future.

It's a good idea to have members sign up to a series of commitments, and they might include:

- adjusting their diary to make sure they regularly attend meetings;
- setting goals they want to achieve;
- taking the actions they say they will;
- keeping things confidential.

At the first meeting you will also want to agree the future venue and schedule for meetings.

It's also a good idea for everyone to exchange contact details. It's also good practice for one person to step forward and take all the email addresses and start an email mailing list so that everyone can stay in touch between meetings – Yahoo Groups offers such a facility, for example.

Manage expectations because everyone needs to understand that there will be a development curve. A good attitude for everyone to have about Masterminding meetings is to imagine that they have paid £1,000 for the privilege of being at each meeting – then they'll always show up prepared to play full on.

It's at the second meeting where Masterminding will really begin, so you will need to set up everyone in terms of the way they'll need to prepare for it and all future meetings.

Specifically, each member needs to produce what we call in Masterminding a blueprint. This is covered in detail in a later chapter, but essentially a blueprint is a detailed description of what people want to achieve by certain dates, namely, in 1 year, 3 year, 5 year and 10 year timeframes.

# Preparing for Masterminding meetings

Ahead of every meeting, out of their blueprint, members need to pick out a goal, a problem or a challenge they want to work on at their next meeting and decide on the precise form of help they're looking for. This is such an important step. It's no good showing up at a meeting having only thought about what you want help with on the way to the meeting.

When a goal or challenge is stated clearly and the type of help wanted is described fully, then the collective energy of the group can be better directed towards providing the help required.

So, as an example, say someone says they have a goal of wanting to earn more money this year than they did last year. If they earned £40,000 last year, then earning £40,001 this year would mean they would have achieved their goal – but that is highly unlikely to have been what they meant by 'earn more'. The phrase 'earn more' is too vague and in this instance, the person should have stated exactly how much they wanted to earn in the year.

It's best if people take at least 30 minutes to think about and write down what the issue they need help with is and email it out to everyone a day or so before the meeting.

## Running Masterminding meetings

Precisely how long each meeting should last depends largely on the number of people in attendance. To do Masterminding justice its best if each person gets at least 15 minutes of Masterminding.

To ensure meetings run smoothly roles need to be assumed by members of the team. A rota should be devised for rotating these roles so that everyone gets a turn at each on a regular basis. One person can, of course, take on more than one role in a meeting if need be.

The roles are as follows.

### Chairperson

The job of the chairperson is to arrange meetings and to control and direct the proceedings when the meetings take place. They will have the authority to keep order and maintain progress in line with the agenda. However, the chairperson is also an important member of the group and must not just stand back but must be active.

The chairperson needs to:

- assume a position of authority if necessary so that control is maintained, that progress is made and that the meeting runs as it should;

- be flexible so as to allow slight deviations that could produce a clarification or the bonding together of meeting participants, for example;

- be responsible so that they are able to accept and work with the broad cross section of personalities that can exist in a team.

Crucially, it is the job of the chair to ensure there is a spirit of cooperation and harmony within the group and that all the other groundrules are being followed.

**The Action Facilitator**

The first job for this person is to fully complete a record sheet for the meeting which should include:

- the date and time of the meeting;
- the venue;
- who attended;
- a summary of the success stories, the issues that were masterminded and the actions that were agreed by each person (both the actions people said they would take in relation to their issue plus the help they offered other team members);
- decisions made.

They should copy this sheet to all members within 1 week of the meeting. The ideal is 48 hours.

This person should be the Chairperson at next event as they produced the action record sheet at the previous meeting.

## Time Keeper

The job of this person is to make sure that meetings run to schedule. Ahead of each meeting, they should check that everyone knows the venue and start time.

People should arrive 10 to 15 minutes before the scheduled start time to ensure a prompt start. If members cannot attend a meeting or if they are going to be late it is the time keeper they should inform.

During the meetings, the time keeper's job is to:

- ensure the meeting starts and ends on time – 2 hours is a good 'rule of thumb' for meetings but of course individuals can always stay on after that to talk to each other if they choose;

- ensure that every person gets an equal time when they are receiving help – this amount of time will be agreed upfront by the group but will always be at least 10 minutes. It should normally be in the 15 – 20 minutes range;

- the time keeper should watch the clock and give an alert 2 minutes before the end of the allotted slots and when time is up.

## The agenda

There are two types of Masterminding meeting: structured and freestyle. In the structured format, everyone turns up with the issue they want to work on already in mind and is allocated a certain amount of time in which they will be masterminded.

In a freestyle format, the meeting is more casual but still works to the same agenda. People still need to arrive with their issues in mind that but no time limits are assigned to each person and a conversation is allowed to drift onto different subjects depending on the mood of the group. This is because going off on apparent tangents can sometimes lead to the result required.

The suggested agenda for meetings is as follows.

- Welcome and allocation of roles for the meeting
- The Masterminding Blessing
- Positive Start – 2 minutes per person
- Education Slot (optional) – 10 minutes
- Masterminding – 10 to 20 minutes per person
- Agreeing Actions – 2 minutes per person
- Any Other Business – 5 to 10 minutes

After everyone has been welcomed the first item on the agenda should be the Masterminding Blessing. This is, in effect, a form of words read out by the Chair that reminds everyone why they are there:

"We are here today to help each other achieve goals and overcome challenges through Masterminding. We will suggest ideas, provide feedback, encourage and inspire, provide resources and contacts, challenge and hold each other accountable. We will do so in a spirit of harmony, cooperation and collaboration."

Next is the Positive Start. This is where each member shares their success stories: in turn, everyone tells the group what has, or what is going well, right now. This sets a constructive and supporting tone for the rest of the meeting and builds confidence.

The next item on the agenda should be an education slot. This is where members share something they have learnt with the rest of the group. It might be something they've read in a book or something they've picked up on a training course or from their own experience.

Next you should move into the Masterminding section of the meeting. The format should be that every person takes it in turns to receive help from the group. When each person is in the 'hotseat' they are the mastermindee at that point. The people providing the help are the masterminders.

Each mastermindee gets between 10 and 20 minutes. They start out by telling the group the issue they'd like to work on. As briefly and as clearly as they can, they explain the goal, challenge or problem and ask the group for the kind of help they think they need. So, for example, it might be ideas, feedback, contacts, resources, help making a decision, inspiration, support or just to be heard or listened to.

People should not use ambiguous terms in the way that they describe their issue. For example, words like proactive and dynamic are open to interpretation and are often misunderstood. People should use words that are unlikely to be misunderstood or misinterpreted.

In other words, objectives should be stated in a simple, concise and clear way. Detail and background information is fine but should not form part of the description of the objective.

So, for example, in stating their objective someone might say:

- "The goal I am working on is … and the type of help I need is …" or
- "The problem or challenge I am facing right now is and my desired outcome is … and the type of help I need to get there is …"

There should be a spirit of harmony at this point. All masterminders need to be fully committed to helping the mastermindee. The job of the masterminders is to listen very attentively and to check that they fully understand the issue and the type of help required. Masterminders can ask questions to clarify the goal if they need to and challenge the mastermindee to be sure they want what they say they want.

Everyone needs to be clear and it is worth taking the time to make sure this the case. The mind energy will not be focused and powerful if everyone is thinking about how to help the mastermindee achieve a slightly different objective. The power is lessened if everyone is not completely clear. The whole group needs to understand it in the same way.

When everyone is clear, the group needs to switch to using the appropriate Masterminding technique based on the type of help the mastermindee has requested. The techniques are described in a later chapter and include ideastorming, feedbacking, connecting, inspiring and resourcing.

The mastermindee should take lots of notes at this point of the ideas, suggestions, thoughts, contacts, resources and support offered by the group. Another idea is to record this section of the machine on a voice recording machine so that nothing that is said is missed.

Everyone gets a turn to be masterminded and once that's done, the attention switches to the action that people will take based on the help they've been given by the group. Everyone checks through their notes and assigns priorities.

Prioritising is such an important step because so many thoughts come out of Masterminding sessions that you can be overwhelmed. Masterminders should categorise their notes into:

- A – actions they will take within 48 hours
- B – actions they will take within a week
- C – actions they will take within a month
- D – actions they will take someday

They should then, in turn, announce to the group the actions they are committed to taking and when by.

## After the Masterminding meetings

Masterminding without action and follow-up is useless and a terrible waste of time so following through is crucial. There's an old saying that "you have learned nothing until you have a permanent change in results" and that's what Masterminding is all about.

Not following through can be debilitating. People will begin to wonder why they are offering help if they don't see action being taken. Soon they'll wonder why they should continue to offer help. And the answer is they shouldn't. Everything about a Masterminding meeting should move people towards taking action towards their goals.

Masterminding doesn't begin and end with the meetings. Knowing from the meetings what kind of help and support each member needs, people should stay in touch and provide help and assistance to each other as and when they can on an ongoing basis.

What happens ultimately with Masterminding is that each member of the team thinks about the needs and desires of each other on a daily basis and their minds become permanently tuned into how they can help their fellow Masterminding team members.

"The big secret in life is that there is no big secret. Whatever your goal, you can get there if you're willing to work."

Oprah Winfrey

# MASTERMINDING TECHNIQUES

There are a variety of techniques that facilitate the Masterminding process. They can be categorised into:

- **Individual Masterminding skills** that people will use outside of the meetings, for example, to prepare for forthcoming get-togethers

- **Masterminding meeting techniques** to be used to help masterminders and mastermindees get better results during the Masterminding phase of meetings

- **Masterminding procedure techniques** that assist with the process of running the meetings

Let's look at each technique in turn.

## Individual Skills

### Blueprinting

In architectural terms a blueprint is a "plan of a building in such detail as to enable workmen to construct it from the print."

With Masterminding you need to give your brain and your Masterminding partners a similarly complete, clear, and vivid description of what you want to create for your life or in business. This blueprint will provide your brain and your Masterminding partners with the help and information they need to help you get there.

"Before you begin a thing, remind yourself that difficulties and delays quite impossible to foresee are ahead. If you could see them clearly, naturally you could do a great deal to get rid of them but you can't. You can only see one thing clearly and that is your goal. Form a mental vision of that and cling to it through thick and thin."

Kathleen Norris, American Novelist

In effect, blueprinting is the bringing together of all your goals into a detailed picture of what your life will be like in 1, 3, 5, 10 and 20 years from now.

The first step is to create your goals in all areas of your life. You need definite, precise and clear goals in order to realise your potential. If you either do not have goals, or if the ones you do have are vague and ambiguous, then you will be like a ship without a rudder. You will be drifting and not steering your ship.

Many people confuse activity with accomplishment. They are busy but, because they're not working towards achieving precise goals, they do not accomplish anything like as much as they could.

When people say they don't have the time to reach their goals, this is not true – it's not time they lack but direction. If you know where you're going then you're going to achieve more and be much more efficient with the use of your time. With definite goals you release your own power.

**You must set 'heartfelt' goals**

If this process is to work the goals you set that form your blueprint must be heartfelt ones. They must be goals that you genuinely want to achieve.

To do this you need to dream like a child. Most adults never define their heartfelt goals. So, in this respect, children are wiser as they know what they want, aren't afraid to ask and never give up until they get it. For example, if a child wants an ice cream and his or her mother says: "No you can't, that's not a good idea," the child will simply say "OK I'll have chocolate instead then."

"Imagination is the beginning of creation. You imagine what you desire, you will what you imagine and at last you create what you will."

George Bernard Shaw

If we think of life as a journey in a car then the direction of our journey is our heartfelt goals and our intentions. Our desires are the most powerful driver of our lives – both physically and spiritually.

Often we are confused and we become clearer when we are angry, sad or happy. Most of the time, we are confused about our heartfelt goals because life seems to be directionless and unsatisfying. We are without aims and direction. Sometimes we are happy and sometimes not. We do not understand all the confusion.

As we grow older we tend not to ask for what we want and so we become aimless. You need to understand that the doorway to the magic in life lies in our aims and intentions. Why does this happen as we grow older?

One reason is conditioning, which places limits on what people believe is possible for them to achieve. In the 1940s, for example, running a four minute mile was thought to be beyond the physical limits of the human body. However, on May 6, 1954, Roger Bannister thought differently and ran the first sub-four-minute mile in recorded history at 3 minutes, 59.4 seconds.

The mental and physical barrier had been broken and six weeks later the Australian athlete, John Landy, followed in Bannister's footsteps and ran a 3:58 mile, breaking Bannister's record.

"Hope begins in the dark, the stubborn hope that if you just show up and try to do the right thing, the dawn will come. You wait and watch and work: You don't give up."

Anne Lamott, American Novelist

Over 50 years on, what was once thought to be impossible has now been achieved by many athletes and is now the standard by which all professional middle distance runners are measured.

So why is then that children have no problem deciding what they want and believing that anything is possible, yet so many adults have a hard time doing the same thing? One reason is the ego. Your ego is your vision of who you are and what you can do. As children, our ego has not been fully established so we are able to discover our desires and we are also able to articulate what they are very quickly.

Ego is the device that tells us that we are different. The role of ego – its true purpose if you like – is to allow us to enjoy the diversity of life such as different kinds of people and the seasons of the year. But the ego can get out of hand. It is a template. It is like a window on our understanding based on our own experiences and our DNA. Ego is our template for perceiving reality. If we utilize ego properly we can enjoy life and different experiences, however, too strong an ego means that we can end up pre-judging things.

If a goal is not from the heart but emanates from the mind, the intellect or the ego then it is not a heartfelt desire. If you set a heartfelt goal there is no way it cannot become a reality. Heartfelt goals are why we are here. We are here to fulfil our heartfelt desires.

You may be very busy with your life but you should always ask for what you want by setting goals. It is not selfish to do so. Always ask for what you want no matter how difficult it may seem to do so.

## First you must dream

So you need to dream to discover what you really want to achieve in general terms. Then you need to turn the individual goals into a detailed blueprint for each of the timelines.

You need to dream like a child without limits and with total belief. It is only when you have finished dreaming that you should give any thought to how you might achieve your goals. It is only when you have completed that stage that you need to evaluate your goals.

The sequence here is important. This is the process that Walt Disney used to go through. Too often, people think about the 'how' and the potential pitfalls of a goal before they have first finished building and picturing their dream.

So how do you know if the goals you have set are not what you truly want? Surely if they've come to you as thoughts they must be what you truly want? Not necessarily. Think about it. Some thoughts and opinions you have didn't start out as your own. They were the thoughts and opinions of other people and so it is sometimes with your goals. You may think they are your own heartfelt goals when in fact they are not.

Clues that goals you have set are not heartfelt and what you truly want include:

- not feeling excited or enthused when you think about them

- feeling tired or burnt out when you try to work towards achieving them

We tend to not set the goals we would like to achieve but instead we set ones that we think are possible. It is our rational, logical mind rather than the creative part of our mind that does this kind of limited thinking. Our logical mind bases its judgments on what it sees around it so, therefore, tends to set goals based on our past achievements and the world around us.

When you feel what you really want and set it as a definite goal, you set energy in motion. Setting a very specific objective backed with emotional desire sets the wheels in motion for the realisation of that goal.

## Think big

You should think big and should not limit yourself. Ask yourself, what do I really want? Forget about what you think you want or what your friends, family or society says you should want. What do you really, really want? You're going to get a result anyway and it is as likely to be a big result as a small one, so why not think big?

Unlike most people you know or will meet, your Masterminding group will not ridicule you for thinking big.

There is excitement in setting big goals. When you set goals – and particularly large ones – something inside of you says "Let's go" and creates excitement. If you make your goals big and tough then you will perform better. Small goals do not have the same capacity to stir your soul.

The way you see life and yourself will largely determine what you get out of it – so set precise and big goals and you're more than half way towards accomplishing them.

"Everything you can imagine is real."

Pablo Picasso

Also if you don't have large, exciting and long-range goals then the short-term obstacles you may meet along the way will be needlessly frustrating.

Many people don't set big goals because they've been disappointed at not achieving goals they've set in the past. Often they lay the blame for that on the fact that the goals they set were 'unrealistic'.

The actual reasons why people fail to achieve their goals normally centre around trying to achieve on their own without the help of others and the fact that the goals were not what the truly wanted.

Another mistake that people often make in their thinking is to fall into the "if I don't set big goals then I won't end up being disappointed when I don't achieve them" trap. This fear of disappointment leads to people setting goals that are just a bit more than they have now. They seem 'realistic' and are not too disappointing if not achieved.

Some people are also afraid to set big goals for fear of being ridiculed by their friends and family. This is one of the beauties of Masterminding because your partners will not ridicule you for having high ambition. In fact, they will provide you with the belief that you may need.

When you set your goals remember to ask for their achievement or something better. This means being flexible because you may end up achieving something much bigger and much better.

"We find no real satisfaction or happiness in life without obstacles to conquer and goals to achieve."

Maxwell Maltz, Cosmetic Surgeon and the
developer of Psycho-Cybernetics

### How to set heartfelt goals

Remember, when setting goals, you should think like a child – in other words, without limits. Take this process seriously because goals casually set are freely abandoned at the first obstacle.

To set your heartfelt goals put some dedicated time aside when you are feeling relaxed. Ask yourself the question: what would I really love to have and do with my life?

Some people have a problem with answering this question. They know what they don't want but not what they do want. Often what they want is the opposite of what they don't want and this process is useful because it requires you to identify what you don't want initially.

So take each area of your life that you want to work on and go through the following process.

### *Step 1 – Get real*

Describe how your life in the area is right now. Express the good, bad and the ugly because you need to get to the core and essence of what is troubling you. This step will give you the insights into what you need to do turn to things around.

### *Step 2 – Clear out time*

What do you want to get rid of? This is your opportunity to really have a rant. Clear the decks.

"Our lives improve only when we take
chances – and the first and most
difficult risk we can take is to be
honest with ourselves."

Walter Anderson

### Step 3 – What do you want?

Take a new piece of paper and at the top of the page write the words 'what I want'. Then start to write down whatever comes out. Do not hesitate or question what comes out. Just write and write as fast as you can. Next, answer the question 'what makes me think I can't have the things I've written down?' Write down all the reasons why you think you can't have what you want. Write down all the obstacles, beliefs and difficulties that come to mind, both large and small.

### Step 4 – Why do you want what you want?

This is all the emotional stuff – the reasons why you want what you want. What feelings will the achievement of your goals give you?

### Step 5 – What has to change?

Finally, answer the question 'what will have to change in order for me to get what I want?' The willingness to change is the key. You may not have to in the end, but the willingness is to do so is crucial.

### Turn your goals into a detailed Blueprint

Take your list of goals and think about when you'd like to achieve them by. Decide which ones you want to achieve within 1 year, within 3 years, within 5 years, within 10 years and within 20.

Be very specific with your goals and describe them in as much detail as you can. Visualise your goals as if they were already achieved. See yourself reaching them – in minute detail, describe in writing what it will be like when you have achieved your goals.

Next, identify the milestones that you will achieve along the way and the obstacles you are likely to face. In other words, work back and identify what would have to happen or what would have to be achieved in order for your goals to be met. The purpose of doing this is to help you to understand and be ready for the challenges and milestones that you will have to reach along the way.

So if, for example, you set a goal to start a new business and achieve a turnover of £300,000 in the first year, what would have to happen in order to get there?

Turn all of this information into a detailed blueprint of what your life will be like having achieved these goals in the timeframes you have set.

Then look at your one year goals and go down a level further and turn these goals into monthly goals. As you work throughout the year, turn these monthly goals into weekly and daily goals and actions.

If you do not turn goals into this level of detail, then you will end up being no more than a dreamer. Plus, achieving the short-term goals also gives you confidence which is precisely what you need when you're shooting for big goals. Confidence is the hallmark of success and it will build and build as you achieve your smaller goals.

**Share your Blueprint**

So once you're ready, it helps to tell others about your Blueprint and the goals it consists of. However, do not share with people who do not believe in you and who do not want you to achieve your ambitions. This is one of the beauties of the Masterminding process – your fellow team members will believe in you.

Your Masterminding team will help you to achieve your goals. When you share your goals with them they will help you in many ways such as ideas for overcoming obstacles and making sure you take the actions necessary.

Think again about how an aeroplane stays constantly fixed on its target of landing at an airport and adjusts as it flies so that it ends up zeroing in towards its destination. That's what you must do. Never take your eyes off your goals. Your aim should be to seek a sense of momentum because when you build up a head of steam, you crash through obstacles that are in your way.

**Picturing**

Your Blueprint is your written description of what you want to achieve and the next step is to 'picture' your goals in your head as this facilitates the Masterminding process.

Imagine what things will be like when you have achieved your goals. Paint a picture of that in your mind in exquisite detail. Make this vision a multi-sensory experience so, as best you can, hear the sounds, feel the feelings, and taste and smell what the outcome you are seeking will be like once achieved.

"In the absence of clearly-defined goals, we become strangely loyal to performing daily trivia until ultimately we become enslaved by it."

Robert Heinlein, Author

Picturing will achieve a number of things. First of all, it will help you to explain your goal to your Masterminding partners. They will be able to more effectively help you when they can visualise, appreciate and understand what your goal looks like as well as you do. Clarity is power.

Secondly, your subconscious mind doesn't know the difference between what is real and what is imagined. So if you picture yourself as having already achieved your desire, the mind will get to work on making it a reality.

To help, you can either:

- buy a scrapbook and fill it with pictures that depict your dreams from newspapers, magazines or from the Internet

- create a collage of images from the Internet and make this picture the desktop image on your computer

- create a PowerPoint presentation or some other image bank on your computer or phone

## Imprinting

The more often you can remember and picture your Blueprint, the more likely it is to become a reality. The challenge is that we can get so caught up in daily life that we forget about what really matters.

Imprinting is a way of reaffirming and burning that image into your mind so that it is with you all the time. It is a form of mental rehearsal.

"Do something. If it doesn't work, do something else. No idea is too crazy."

Jim Hightower, Activist

A way to do it is to start your day by going on a mental journey. Choose a short walk that you take on a frequent basis – for example, your journey to the local shops or the train station. Choose 4 landmarks on that journey – for example, houses you pass, corners you take or shops you pass. Then take your 1, 3, 5, 10 and 20 year blueprints and imagine that you are stepping into those places when you reach those landmarks. Picture them vividly in your mind.

The beauty of this technique is that when you take that walk for real in the future those images will come to you as you pass the landmarks, thereby helping to imprint what you want to achieve into your mind.

**Emotionalising**

Putting emotion behind your goals is also crucially important. The stronger the emotion behind a thought, the faster the results will be achieved. This means being clear on why you want to achieve the goal.

What are the emotions you will feel when you achieve the goal and what are the ones you will no longer feel? Emotion is the energy that drives you. It is the fuel you need for the journey so you should emotionalise your goals on a daily basis.

# Masterminding Meeting Techniques

### Ideastorming

When a team member says they are looking for ideas, the job of the masterminders is to take the lid of their thinking in a process known as ideastorming.

"Everyone is a genius at least once a year. The real geniuses simply have their bright ideas closer together."

Georg Christoph Lichtenberg, German Scientist

These are the rules for ideastorming:

- The mastermindee in the 'hot seat' should start out by – as clearly as they can – setting out the issue they want ideas in respect of. If any of the masterminders are unclear they should seek clarification at this stage.

- A time limit should be set.

- Before the idea generation session begins the mastermindee should adopt a positive physiology (for example, sitting up straight) and the masterminders should all match the physiology of the mastermindee as much as is possible.

- After a few quiet moments to think, masterminders should then all take it in turns to offer an idea.

- There should be no criticism or judgment from anyone at this stage.

- All ideas should be welcomed no matter how silly or far out they seem. In fact, the mastermindee should say "thank you" every time an idea is offered.

- The more ideas the better because at this point you don't know what might work.

- Absolutely no discussion should take place during the idea generation session. Talking about the ideas will take place afterwards.

- The mastermindee should not comment and should spend their time writing down all the ideas offered.

"Every composer knows the anguish
and despair occasioned by forgetting
ideas which one had no time
to write down."

Hector Berlioz, French Composer

- Masterminders should never hesitate even if someone has an idea which may seem stupid or unrelated they should say it anyway. It may turn out to be a missing piece in the jigsaw later on.

- Ideas should never be ridiculed because they may trigger someone else to come up with an even better idea.

- Ideas should flow at a rapid pace. The pressure should be on for people to keep coming up with ideas because the logical and rational mind tends to dominate over the creative mind. The logical and rational mind will step in if the flow starts to slow down.

- Ideas should never be rejected because the resources don't currently exist for making the idea happen because the resources may be available at a later date.

**Feedbacking**

Feedbacking is a process for providing a response or view on a situation that enables that situation to be improved.

The way feedback is provided determines whether or not it has the desired impact. One of the aims should be to make sure a defensive response from the person receiving the feedback is avoided.

Feedbacking should elicit a positive response from the person it is offered to. If there is no change, then feedback is just 'noise'.

"Feedback is the breakfast
of champions."

Ken Blanchard, Author
of 'The One Minute Manager'

Here are some tips on how to do that.

- Feedback is observations, views and information – it is not advice in the form of "If I were you I'd …" or "You shouldn't have done that …"

- Ask 'What if …?' questions.

- When providing feedback make sure it is honestly geared to helping the person. In other words, be constructive. Constructive feedback is not criticism but is descriptive.

- Don't be personal – talk about the behaviour the person exhibited and not their personality or motivations.

- Mention things that someone can do something about and not things that are out of their control.

- Get the timing right – feedback is best delivered as close to the event in question or time it was requested as possible.

- Do not question intentions or motivations when providing feedback – that normally provokes the defensive response you're trying to avoid.

### Connecting and resourcing

In Masterminding, people often need contacts, information, data and other resources to move forward with a goal or with solving a problem and its amazing how often fellow masterminders are able to provide that.

Six degrees of separation is the theory that anyone on earth can be connected to any other person on the planet through a chain of acquaintances that has no more than five intermediaries. The theory was first proposed in 1929 by the Hungarian writer Frigyes Karinthy.

Every time you meet in a Masterminding setting the chances are very high that you know someone who can help any of your fellow masterminders with their goals or challenges. Think of that often because if contacts are not generated at every single Masterminding meeting then something is wrong.

Every time an idea is generated the question should be 'who knows someone or something that can help with this idea or issue?' People in the Masterminding group should be willing to share their contacts and resources.

Tips for when doing the asking:

- Instead of asking for contacts or resources in a vague way, be very specific. Create a clear and very specific picture of the kind of person or information you are looking for.

- If you're looking for a contact, clearly state how you'd like the introduction to happen. For example, would you like your team member to set up a meeting or lunch between the three of you or do you want their permission to use their name when you call?

- Be clear on the ways in which what you have in mind would be beneficial to the contact you are seeking – 'what's in it for them' basically.

- Thank the person who provides you with the contact and make sure you follow through and report back on how it went.

Tips for when being asked for contacts or resources:

- Be organised with your contact list and, ideally, bring it with you to your Masterminding meeting.
- Do what you can to lay the ground for all parties and facilitate introductions and meetings if that would help.
- In the early days, if you're not that familiar with the person being masterminded and do not want to handover your contact's details just yet, offer to contact the person you know first and get their permission to be contacted.
- Always seek to provide quality contacts, ideally, people you can personally vouch for.
- Expand your thinking to include contacts that your contacts
- If you are given a contact, make sure you follow up on it. When you have done so, get back in touch with the person who gave you the contact to say thank you. This will encourage them to help you again in the future.

**Reporting**

Reporting is about being accountable to yourself and to your Masterminding team. So how do you hold yourself and the members of your Masterminding team accountable without upsetting anyone?

Here's what not to do:

- tell people what their actions should be
- tell people how they should report in to the team on what they've agreed to do

"There are people who, instead of listening to what is being said to them, are already listening to what they are going to say themselves."

Albert Guinon, French Playwright

That way suggests a lack of faith and trust in them on your part. Believe in them and do not let them resist the responsibility.

When there is trust and faith, this is what happens:

- people draft their own action lists;
- people tell you what support they need from you plus how often and in what form they will report-in to the team;
- people have clarity on the consequences of not following through.

As a Masterminder your role is to be a supportive servant rather than a policeman.

### Listening

Active listening is a technique for listening and responding to someone that improves understanding. It is crucial to the effectiveness of Masterminding.

Often when people listen, they do so with the intent to respond and not to fully understand. Often they half listen, distracted by their surroundings or thinking about something else.

Active listening is structured. The listener is attentive and listens to the speaker fully and then repeats in their own words what they think the speaker has said. If the speaker thinks that the listener fully understood, the conversation moves on. If not, they attempt to explain themselves again.

### Deciding

Often in Masterminding, people need help deciding on alternative courses of action. Many people make decisions quickly, in the absence of much in the way of information and

"Life shrinks or expands in proportion
to one's courage."

Anais Nin, French Author

with very little thought. The following are techniques that provide a structured way of thinking about, analysing and making decisions and can be used in Masterminding sessions when people say they need help deciding what to do.

## PMI

This is a technique devised by Edward de Bono. What you do is to list the plus, minus, and interesting points. The interesting points are, for example, the consequences of a decision, the uncertainties or even the factors that are neutral.

Much like Masterminding, don't be fooled by the apparent simplicity of this technique. It is very powerful and much neglected.

Most people make decisions before they've weighed up the evidence. They decide either based on emotion or simple logic and then look at the evidence to support their decision. They do it backwards. By considering the evidence on all sides of the situation first, better quality decisions are made.

### Buriden's Ass

So what do you do when the alternatives available are equally attractive? This method is again simple and involves listing only the negative points and all the drawbacks relating to each decision. The reason why this works is because when options seem equally attractive our brains can become blinded to any negatives.

### Measured Criteria

This is a good technique for more complex decisions involving many alternatives. What you do is to draw a table on a piece of paper and list the criteria you want your decision to meet down the side in order of importance. For each of the criteria, you choose a maximum number that you will score your options against based on how important each criterion is to you. Across the top you list your alternatives. You then score each of your alternatives against the criteria.

For example, say you want to buy a new car and there are 3 models that you want to choose between.

You might do it like this.

| Factor | Possible points | Model X | Model Y | Model Z |
|--------|-----------------|---------|---------|---------|
| Price | 50 | 45 | 35 | 30 |
| Comfort | 40 | 30 | 35 | 25 |
| Style | 30 | 10 | 20 | 30 |
| Safety | 20 | 15 | 20 | 10 |
| Total | 140 | 100 | 110 | 95 |

So, in this example, you'd choose Model Y.

## Masterminding Procedure Techniques

As powerful as teamworking is, the reality is that working in a group can, at times, lead to friction and even conflict.

You shouldn't be put off by this because the upsides far outweigh the downsides. You just need to be aware of the fact and know how to deal with it when problems crop up.

When people work in teams there are two difference issues at work. The first is the job to be done and the problems involved along the way, and the second is the process of the group work. The process is the mechanisms through which the team acts as one unit.

Unfortunately not enough attention is normally given to the process. The focus is often on the task at hand. However, without proper attention to the process the results of a group working together are very much lessened.

Clear management of the process, on the other hand, can significantly improve the results achieved and can lead to synergy.

With Masterminding what you need to achieve is a group process which creates a spirit of cooperation, harmony, coordination and widely understood procedures and practices. An effective team exhibits high performance and high levels of mutual support, both practical and moral.

Team working enables the full use of the talents available, however, all teams take a while to settle in and go through four distinct stages, which are:

- **Forming** occurs when any team is first organized. At this stage, needs and questions occur in the minds of the team members. Group members at this stage often have high expectations as well as anxiety about where they individually will fit in. That's why 'icebreakers' are such a good idea at the forming stage and why it is good to assign roles to people.

- **Storming** will probably not last long but is when group members can sometimes rebel against each other and often against authority. Members may express disappointment with lack of progress. This is when consensus building and conflict resolution can be required.

- **Norming** occurs when teams successfully resolve the storming issues. Dissatisfaction is replaced by harmony, trust, support, and respect. Group members are more open and willing to provide feedback.

- **Performing** is the stage you are aiming for as it is when the group will be highly productive. You will be working in harmony, collaboratively and interdependently.

For a group of individuals to form into a self-managed and cohesive unit two main sets of skills need to be acquired. They are managerial and interpersonal. The faster these skills are acquired, the faster the team develops. For example, meetings need to be organised, rules must be set.

To accelerate group development, a good practice is to have a facilitator whose role is to manage the group process and to improve the group skills. It is best if this role is rotated around the group.

Other good practices are as follows.

**Focus**

This helps in terms of decision-making and conflict resolution. The rule is that group decisions are made by the group and not individuals. This also applies to problem solving whereby it is best if the group solves the problem. If there is conflict then it should be considered in terms of the task.

## Clarification

Clarity is of paramount importance. If an individual is performing something and only understands the task to a level of 75%, imagine if every member of a 5-person team understands it to the same level of 75%, then the misunderstanding is multiplied and the chances of success are much reduced. So clarity is crucial. The first responsibility of the group is to clarify the task and write it down so that everyone can see it.

## The quiet one

Invariably in any group, there is someone who doesn't say very much. It is the duty of that individual to speak up and it is the job of the group to encourage and include this person.

## The dominant one

Also, in any group, there is often a talkative person who has a tendency to take over proceedings. It is the task of that person to quieten down and listen more and it is the responsibility of the group to ask that person to personally take a hand in eliciting the views of other people.

## Written records

Decisions which are not clearly and concisely recorded will get lost and often end up being discussed again, usually at length.

## Feedback

It should be a rule that criticisms are neutral and are focused on the task and not the person. Every negative criticism should be accompanied by a positive suggestion for improvement and positive actions should be praised.

### Handling failure

Failures should not be ignored but, instead, should be examined for the causes and ways to avoid a repetition should be sought.

### Handling deadlock

When two or more opposing points of view are held then something has to be done otherwise a standstill will result. One way is for the different camps to talk about the other point of view in an attempt to understand it better. This in itself may result in a resolution and, if not, another strategy is to look for common ground in light of the original objective.

### Losing sight

In discussions sometimes the larger picture can be obscured and often it is useful to remind people of the target.

# AUTHOR PROFILES

### ARTHUR MAGOULIANITI
**www.arthurmagoulianiti.com**

Arthur Magoulianiti is a High Performance Coach and Consultant to Individuals and Businesses helping Clients operate at significantly increased levels of both effectiveness and efficiency which leads to extraordinary achievements and results.

Having had a successful career in Corporate IT, Arthur followed his dream of being self-employed and moved into Property in 2004. He went on to create a 7 figure property portfolio in just over 5 years, becoming financially independent and creating his ideal lifestyle which now includes living on the Mediterranean Island of Cyprus. Having achieved great success with his property business, Arthur followed his passion for personal development to become a certified Coach, Trainer, Speaker and Founding Partner of the John Maxwell Team, the No 1 training and coaching group in the world with regards to Leadership and now coaches and speaks with clients around the world.

Masterminding, as a concept and strategy, has been fundamental to my success to date both with my property business and now with my coaching business, where the results I have been fortunate to attain, in a short period of time, has been down to masterminding with some of the most talented and gifted entrepreneurs and teachers in both industries.

## MAC ATTRAM
**www.MacAttram.com**

Mac Attram (MBA) is the Multi-Award Winning co-founder of SalesPartners UK; a Business Coaching, Consulting & Training Company, which helps business owners increase sales, maximise profits and build winning business teams.

Mac is an accomplished millionaire serial entrepreneur, business consultant and international speaker. He is also the author of *'The Inspired Warrior's Code'*.

Mac has been involved in training and coaching over 40,000 people around the world and has shared the stage with some of the world's premier thought-leaders and speakers, including Robert Kiyosaki, T.Harv Eker, Blair Singer, Les Brown & Keith Cunningham.

He has been featured as an expert advisor across a string of media platforms, including Sky TV, The Guardian, The Huffington Post, VOX Africa & Real Business Magazine.

Mac has known for many years that his life mission is to inspire, educate and empower people to live a life of joy, courage, passion and purpose. The testimonials that he receives demonstrate that Mac is living his mission, and aiding thousands to accomplish their life and business mission in the process.

He has been a disciplined Black Belt teacher and student (for over 30 years) in the martial art of TaeKwondo in which he is a former national champion.

He is married to Linda and they have 3 young children.

Feel free to get in touch.

### KARL PEARSALL

Karl is the founder of Yes Group Worldwide. Established in 1993, it is Europe's leading volunteer personal development organisation.

Meeting every month for over 20 years, The Yes Group is an institution with a list of speakers which reads like a "Who's Who" of personal development. It also has a great heritage in its leadership including co-author of this book, Mac Attram, who lead the organisation for two years.

Growth and contribution are at its core. Founder Karl Pearsall continues to serve on the board of the Community Interest Company pushing its charitable and social impact objectives. Karl's efforts in London have led to more groups in other cities, and further throughout Europe and beyond. Find out more at **www.yesgroup.org.**

Karl's primary business since 1999 is a merchandising and branding company that imports and decorates promotional items. Through a masterminding connected network, Original Thing (**www.OriginalThing.com**) serves blue chip clients, professional organisations, boutique hotels and other five star venues.

Along with this legacy customer base, Karl serves a niche he calls 'Cause Marketing' as a socially conscious entrepreneur. Karl blogs and shares how to promote and fundraise for good causes. Discover more at **BrandMyTribe.com.**

Taking this to another level in the form of a Mastermind consultancy, Karl helps leaders grow, build and lead their tribe.

Discover more at **MastermindYourTribe.com.**

Please get in touch if you think Karl can be of service on any of the above with your goals and cause by emailing him on **karl@karlpearsall.com.**

Please visit Karl's LinkedIn profile or follow him on Twitter – **@karlpearsall.**

- Karl says about Masterminding that he has more than one peer group. Always fluid and focused on particular outcomes, vitality, business, selling, leadership, relationship. That's why he still values highly what we created together, and that's he still shares the ideas and skills this book is founded on.

- Karl's skill set revolves around events people communications branding both corporate and personal, being at the forefront of revolutions; dance music, personal development, the NLP, coaching, expert and collaboration revolutions.

- Karl provides keynote talks on personal leadership, masterminding, and branding.

## STEVE W ROCHE

Steve runs Wizeeka, which provides thinking skills training and innovation consultancy services.

He is the author of the book *The MultipleMind Method.*

Steve runs his own mastermind group called The Ideas Crowd (**www.ideascrowd.com**).

**Notes from the authors about Masterminding**

- You may come across the term 'Mastermind Groups'. They are not to be confused with what we have described in this book. There is a major difference between how they work and the process we call Masterminding®. Mastermind Groups are different in the sense that they are normally lead by experts in a particular field and the focus is on the teaching of specific content.

- Since we developed the peer-to-peer Masterminding mindset, skillset and process the founders have built and delivered a training to mirror it and trained entrepreneurs, school teachers, key people of influence, and property developers amongst others. Get in touch if you are seeking to learn or create a group via: **www.masterminding.net.**

- We believe that it's good to have strong peer groups in life, and to learn from everyone.

- Discover more about the authors and your how to have your own Masterminding group by visiting **masterminding.net.**

# "Act as if it were impossible to fail."

Dorothea Brande, Writer and Editor

Printed in Great Britain
by Amazon